Keeping It *100*

A Young Woman's Guide to Personal Growth

NINA MICHELLE

KEEPING IT *100*

Copyright © 2016 by Nina Michelle
All rights reserved.

Published by:
NyreePress Literary Group
Fort Worth, TX 76161
1-800-972-3864
www.nyreepress.com

All rights reserved. No part of this book may be used or reproduced by any means, graphic, electronic, or mechanical, including photocopying, recording, taping or by any information storage retrieval system without the written per- mission of the publisher. Copying this book is both illegal and unethical.

ISBN print: 978-0-9972921-7-6

Library of Congress Control Number: pending

Inspiration / Women's Inspiration

Printed in the United States of America

Dedication

I would like to dedicate this book to God! It is because of His will and purpose that I am even able to put the words together to write this book. This has been a journey and a process; I am beyond elated to see it come to fruition. God dropped this book into my spirit in June of 2013 at 6:39 a.m. It has been a long road but, because of His grace and mercy, I have finished. I want to thank my children for being the motivation to not give up. I want to thank my friend for believing in me and telling me to hurry up and write, because "that's a hot title." I want to thank my family for supporting me, and I want to thank life for the lessons, experiences, and circumstances to even have the background for a book like this!

Contents

Introduction 7

You are NOT a statistic! 11

Expectation vs. Reality 17

You Gotta Stop Living A Lie 23

The Baby is Not the End 27

Say NO to the Influence of Drugs 33

Sex or No Sex: That Is the Question ... 41

Coming Out the Closet 47

Alone in a crowded room 51

Finding the God in Me 57

Walking in Purpose 61

Introduction

I believe this book can fall into so many categories. It is hard to define just exactly what type of read this is. If it is nothing else, it is REAL on every level, and it attempts to discuss the things that people "feel", but never really want to talk about.

My hope is that the book makes you laugh, cry, reflect, and find purpose. This book will give you experiences to relate to so you can know that you are NOT alone. Most importantly, my goal is for this book is to give you inspiration to change your status in life! The status is not reflective only of how other people view you, but also of how you view yourself!

My hope is that the book gives you the will to fight when all you can see is failure. There will be moments in this book where there is no explanation for the success, accomplishments, or the overcoming of obstacles. In these moments in this book you will see nothing else BUT GOD! There cannot be credit given to anyone else but God.

I don't want to make this a long drawn out book because people have things to do in life. But, if you take the time to read this book it is sure to help, or at least get you fueled up enough to do something different. You are not what society is trying to make you become! You are what God predestined you to be before he laid the foundations of the Earth.

I know that the pressures of the world can feel like a million tons of weight on your shoulders. Everyone around you is engaged in things that seem "exciting"—your friends with the weave down their backs, having sex with multiple men to ease the pain of the lack of self-love, drinking lean, and popping pills to numb the consciousness of knowing what you're engaging in is wrong.

Other things like sleeping with other women, because it is presented "as the thing" to do. Or, getting surgery on Care Credit with a fake social security number just to have a flat stomach, fat butt, and bigger breasts, only to be fondled and used by a man who pretends to love you until your lease is up, the money is gone, or another girl comes along with more money, a bigger crib, and the willingness to do more sexually than you!

So, you dive deeper into the ditch convincing yourself that this is what you want when, in reality, you've known from the beginning that it is wrong. You don't really love that man, you love the thought of him, but you feel as if you're in so deep you can't possibly give up now! You gave too much of yourself—physically, emotionally, and financially! Please believe me, you can turn the situation around and get back to the essence of who you REALLY are!

Get yourself to a quiet space. Make sure you have enough time to calm yourself. Take a few breaths and just sit there quietly. Don't get up from that space until you start to feel weights being lifted off of you. Read this book and every time you see "But God" I want you to pray this simple prayer: 'God I repent! I accept you as my Lord and Savior, and ask that You rebuild me to be the woman that YOU want me to be!'

You are NOT a statistic!

Coming from a single parent home seems to be a story that is retold frequently. In my community and many communities alike, the majority of families are single parent homes. Usually what comes to mind is a mother with her children struggling to make ends meet. Well, that's not always the case. There are some single parent homes where the father has sole custody of his children. Either way, coming from a single parent home begins what most deem as the beginning of "statistichood". (For the purpose of this book, this word means the state of being a static).

Coming from a single parent family has grave disadvantages. My mother worked endless jobs with long hours in order to provide basic needs. I know most of you can relate to this. Seeing your parent struggle to pay the rent, buy clothes and shoes, and even just to buy food. If you haven't seen this, per say, you don't understand the feeling of lack: not having enough to get by—sleeping three to a twin-sized bed with no sheets, or not knowing where your next meal will come from.

I can remember, vividly, standing at a checkout counter with my mother counting pennies, nickels, and dimes to buy a bag of beans so that we were able to eat! I can remember the look of disgust on the cashier's face, because she had to count all of the change my mother had given her. With every move of a coin during her count the cashier sighed deeply! Every time the cashier sighed, my mother cringed, and she looked as if she was slowly disappearing. She seemed to get smaller and smaller with every moment. I know my mom wanted to run away and hide when we left that store with the shortest receipt I had ever seen. I grabbed the bag, and when we got into the car, my Mom put her head on that steering wheel and cried. She cried as if her soul were leaving her body. She cried so deeply that I felt her pain.

I felt the deepest remorse for my mother, and I was only 12. From that moment on, I tried to understand what my mother was going through. When I asked for things and she said "NO", I understood that it wasn't because she didn't want me to have it. It was because she COULDN'T. So the pending question here is WHY? Why would I put myself in the same predicament? Why would I want to struggle? Why would I become a product of my environment? Are generational factors guiding principles as to how you will live your life?

In most cases, yes! People become what they have learned because they know NO different. All they know is the struggle—section 8, SNAP benefits, low income housing, and childcare checks. I am in NO way downing this, because we ALL need help, but it IS NOT there for you to survive off of. It is presented as a means of help to get you to the next place in life. The amazing thing though, is that you *can* get to the next stage in life! You can break free of all of the generational factors that have hindered your success.

You don't have to carry around excess baggage. You can drop those loads and free your back from the pain! How, you ask? You have to get up and stop being stagnate! Don't just stay in the same place, doing the same thing, with the same people. You have to believe and profess that you can do all things through Christ!

There is immediate power in the things that you speak. I have talked to countless women and men, young and old, who feel like there is NO WAY OUT! They feel as if they can't go on! They feel as is their present situation is their life's destination. If this is how you feel at this moment in "statistichood", you can change your course now by simply saying two words: BUT GOD!

Expectation vs. Reality

There is NOW this unspoken requirement that you have to be a "Bad B****". The problem with this expectation is that it is not CLEARLY defined or rooted in reality. A "Bad B****" means something different to every person you talk to. Even if you Google the term "Bad B****", there are so many images that are from right field to left field, that you could never pinpoint what exactly is being expected of you!

We see images on television of women classified as these "Bad B******". Usually the women have amazing gym bodies that were store bought, tight clothes, long weaves, colored lipstick, and expensive purses and shoes. Is that the definition of a "Bad B****" that so many women are aggressively searching after? The jury is still out on deliberation in that matter!

What I do know is that the reality of that expectation is unreal for a grown woman. A grown woman, in most regards, has limited resources and limited time, because she is handling RESPONSIBILTY! Grown women can't afford to purchase body parts. For the majority of the girls who do get the money, they have sold a piece of their soul for it, or saved and sacrificed the necessities in life in order to make it happen. I don't know about you, but I will keep my soul, my self-worth, and my pride. I would rather have food, shelter, and clothing, than a big booty, flat stomach, and nice breasts!

Tight clothes, revealing clothes, NO clothes—this is the new trend! But along with this comes yeast infections, disrespect from males, and unwanted verbal and sexual abuse. I can recall going to a club with jeans and a shirt on and feeling "overdressed". Every girl that walked past me had at least one body part showing—breasts, butts, glimpses of vagina, or, for the more "lost", combinations of ALL three! But they all had weave!

Believe me, I'm not at all knocking weave. Weave does serve a purpose for some women. However, it becomes a problem when weave becomes an addiction. Like when, instead of paying your rent or caring for your children, you're buying bundles of hair! Some girls will not pay to further their education, but will pay the same amount for some temporary hair from another country. Girls get so caught up in the hype of what society shows you instead of being who you are—doing what makes you happy! Where are the leaders with their own minds? People just follow the trends instead of being trendsetters.

This brings me to the misguided representation for young girls reflected by colored lipstick. COLORED LIPSTICK IS NOT FOR EVERYBODY! In all honesty, I have had conversations with a lot of men, and they don't even like colored lipstick. We are looking at these celebrities and identifying with them, but we don't understand that, after that photo shoot, they are removing that lipstick. They are just putting it on to make you want to purchase it and, after you buy it, their job is done. They are a little richer and you are in the world mimicking a behavior that they don't even indulge in in their everyday lives!

Expensive purses and shoes are fine. I would be telling a true lie if I said I don't like my share of bags (as we describe them) and shoes. Anybody who knows me personally, knows that I say "I'm not wearing a knock-off ". Knock-offs can be purchased at your local nail shop, beauty shop, or out the trunk of someone's car when you're riding through any given neighborhood.

With that being said, we have to put these purchases into perspective. Our priorities must be in order. You cannot purchase a bag or shoes when you owe the cable company, the electric company, and the gas company. You cannot make these purchases when your children are in need of bare necessities. You cannot make these purchases when you have not made any investments in securing your future. For those of you girls smacking your lips right now thinking: 'I ain't buying my own stuff anyway'—we'll get to that in another chapter. Just keep that look on your face and your lips pooched up for the time being.

So how do we defy the expectations that society has put on our lives? Dare to define your own expectations rooted in reality. Look deeply into who you are and who you want to be. Take off the make-up, take out the weave, remove your eyelashes, and put on some loose clothes. Put your shoes and bags on the shelf and deal with the essence of yourself. If you don't identify who you are and where you are going, you're going to chase after everybody else's expectation of who you should be. Accept and embrace where you are, then move forward! If you don't know how to move forward, use these two words: BUT GOD!

You Gotta Stop Living A Lie

In the previous chapter, we ended up discussing the girls who couldn't identify with purchasing their own bags and shoes because some dude was doing it for them. I'm almost 100% sure that their eyes rolled to the back of their heads and their lips were smacking at the thought of that. If you're not one of those girls, you're the girl that's thinking 'how is she getting all those bags and shoes?' Well let's be frank here, if we may. Girls do things for those expensive gifts 95% of the time; some of which they disclose to their friends, and most of which they don't! They keep the dirty little secrets to themselves.

The reality of the matter is: you are an RNG. I'm sure you're looking puzzled now, wondering what that means. You are a RIGHT NOW GIRL! You are not the woman who he will take home to his mother because, in his heart, mind, and eyes, you ARE NOT a woman. You are his side chick, his late night booty call, his 'when my woman is tripping' escape, his quick nut, his "fun" that he is using you solely for sex.

Yes, he is buying you expensive gifts because he has the monetary means to do so. If he was broke would he give you his last? If he's going through a struggle, would he confide in you? If he was trying to better himself and change his lifestyle, would he look to you for help? If his mother died, would you be in the top five people he called to be consoled? The answer is probably no.

You're probably thinking that this doesn't matter, or this is not you because he says he loves you and he comes over or you are over at his place. He might even take you out, have you around the "guys", and you may even incidentally meet his sisters. But do his words match his actions? Is he intentionally trying to know who you are, or are things mostly sexual? He's not lying to you—you are lying to yourself! You are making yourself believe that he loves you, but that is not love. You are using material things to justify your worth. You are living a façade of happiness in life, but when you are all alone in the wee hours of the night, it haunts you. You don't like the woman who you are becoming and you feel lost. You don't even want to associate with these types of friends or dudes anymore, but what else is there to do? First, deal with the truth. The truth is accepting who you are and where you are.

Get a journal and, in those early morning hours, you need to write down the things that haunt you about yourself. This list will be your road map for change. In those early hours, when youare being awakened by feelings of despair, is when God is trying to reach you. He is exposing to you the things that need to be replaced in your life. He is leading you and guiding you to something better. Think about the woman you want to become, accept the truth so you can move forward. If you feel like you can't accept the truth or have no idea where to turn, use these two words: BUT GOD!

The Baby is Not the End

I don't care if you are 10 or 30 when you have a child. The baby is not the end of the road. It is actually a new beginning. Children are a blessing from God. Not every female has the capability to bear children, and if you have had the opportunity to experience this joy, you are blessed beyond measure. Now the truth of the matter is: a baby, while you have no job, no education, no help, and nowhere to turn, is difficult. The reality though, is that it's difficult, but it is NOT impossible. You have got to believe that things will work out for the greater good. You have got to provide an example for that child. Your child should become your motivation to do, and be better.

I personally had a baby before I was ready. I had a very low paying job that I worked when I felt like it. I was not enrolled in school and had absolutely no direction in life. When I found out I was pregnant, I was exactly 9 weeks along, and devastated. I couldn't imagine having another abortion, so I decided to have the baby. I sunk into a depression because I had no idea what was coming next.

I worked my meager job for the next 2 ½ months and then, one day, something happened that entirely changed my life. While sitting in my mother's house trying to decide what I was going to eat, I felt the most amazing thing I have ever encountered in life. My son kicked for the first time. I began to cry hysterically because, it was in that moment that I finally came to terms with the fact that I was responsible for the life of another person. This little boy relied on me for love, support, food, water, clothing, safety, and nurturing. The essence of his success was placed in my hands. He could not be a responsible, respectful, reputable adult without me! I made the decision that day that I had to be more. It wasn't just about me anymore! Someone relied on me for their very existence.

Within the next 2 months, I enrolled in school to begin working on an associate's degree at a city college. It was a long, difficult road. I needed public assistance to make ends meet. I went to school during the day, and worked a couple of nights a week and on the weekend. I rescheduled my life around my son. I worked when someone was able to watch him. I took classes when he had a place to go. My first priority has been and will always be him.

When he turned 2, I graduated from city college with a Liberal Arts degree, and was able to acquire a job as an assistant with the public school system. Was it easy? NO! Was it necessary? Yes, for his survival and mine. There were nights when he wouldn't sleep and I had homework to do. There were nights when sleep never came to me. There were times when I didn't know when or what we would eat. What I never did do, was give up! Two little eyes were looking at me and waiting for my response. Your baby is looking at you too! The last thing you can do is fold.

You have got to know and believe that God makes absolutely no mistakes! He will see you through this situation, but you have GOT to do the work. Yes, it will feel like sometimes that this is the end— but a way will be made. Don't be afraid to ask for help and seek resources from different sources. It is vital to you and your child's success. If you don't have a child yet, please know that, although they are extremely adorable, they come with a plethora of responsibility. Please make sure that you have the right mindset and are on the right path before you embark on such a journey.

As for me, my son is now 10 and is a complete joy. He is everything that I had sacrificed for him to be. He is an honor roll student. He is kind and loving. He cares for other people and has a heart of gold. He shows respect for everyone in his path and is a model young man. Yes, I missed the parties, the out of town trips, the club, and all the "kicking it", but what I acquired was an eternal legacy of greatness! You too can have the same success story, because your baby/babies are not the end—they are the beginning. They are the start of the new you! They are your legacy, and the way you react to them is the way in which they will grow. Formulate a plan. When, where, and what do you want for you and your child/children? What resources do you need? What can you find to help you get there? Once you start to do the work on your path, if you get lost and don't know which way to go, use these two words: BUT GOD!!

Say NO to the Influence of Drugs

Right now, drugs are a very important part of our worldly society. If you turn on television, listen to the radio, or even have small outings with friends—drugs somehow become a part of the conversation. There are a vast variety of drugs that are being widely used by people who are getting younger and younger by the day. People no longer just drink a little alcohol or smoke a little weed. They are popping pills, drinking lean, and lacing their weed.

Not only are these drugs adversely affecting your health young woman, they are altering your decision making process. You are unable to make coherent decisions when you are constantly "waking and baking" or "leaning". This is why you find yourself in situations that are not conducive to success. You may feel like you need to smoke or drink to ease your mind, but I have a better solution. Take that time, energy, and money to do something productive for your future.

The long term effects of drugs on your body are horrendous. You must understand that you are diminishing your brain cells and your capability to bear children at the appropriate time in your life. You are taking God's responsibility into your own hands by shortening your life cycle through using drugs that are affecting your heart, your liver, your lungs, your kidneys, and your brain cells.

You think that it's "cute", but you're aging yourself beyond belief. You want to be on cloud nine, but it's only because you are depressed in real life. You are trying to escape the hurt, the pain, the rejection, the loss of a loved one, having been raped, having been molested when you were a child, having an absent father or a drug addicted mother, a broken heart, or a betrayal by people who you thought were friends. But the drugs DO NOT change the situation.

You will FOREVER try to escape the situation through these means because the drugs don't solve the problem. They just take your mind away until your next "high". What makes you any different than the crackhead on the corner? They are chasing their next "high" also! You are just a "functional" addict. You DO NOT need drugs to have a good time. If you are surrounded by people who need to be "lifted"—FIND A NEW CIRCLE; your life depends on it.

You are figuratively living in darkness. You are being held hostage by drug usage. You are wondering, how? Well let me explain it to you. There are things that God has ordained for you to be doing, but you can't because your mind is not in the right place. You are so busy trying to escape and God is giving you a way out, but you can't hear him! You're listening to the advice of friends who are just as "lost" as you.

You are listening to "trap" music that is encouraging you to turn up. It's influencing you to do things that are not of God. The music is entering your spirit, your friends are influencing your spirit, but it does not belong to them. It belongs to God.

In the previous chapter, I told you about how I received my Associate's Degree after having a baby. At that point in my life, I was building my relationship with God. But, I had one foot in, and one foot out the door. I, admittedly, smoked weed but I was beginning to make some changes. Before I got the job as a teacher's assistant, I was with a circle of friends who would smoke weed daily. I would indulge with them, and we would have "fun".

One particular morning, I received a call to work at a school as a substitute assistant. Right after receiving the call, my "friends" called and said "let's just go smoke and get something to eat". I seriously contemplated the offer, but I knew that I wanted to change. So, I declined and went to work.

My "friends" were disappointed, but from working there that one day, I had received a job offer at that school. I ended up working there for 5 years and made almost triple the income I was making before. What if God had not been leading me to change? What if I wouldn't have gone to work that day? What if I would have chosen the influence of drugs over my future?

I can honestly say that I do not know where I would be today. It was from that job that God placed my passion in me. It was at that job that I met my mentor. It was at that job that I found purpose, and realized that I wanted to be a teacher. It was at that job that I found the strength to go back to school and get a Bachelor's Degree, and two Master's Degrees within a six-year time frame!

What are you missing out on by choosing the influence of drugs over living the life God has for you? Are you missing your purpose because you are too "high"? Are you and your circle of friends productive, or just the life of the party? How can you begin to make a change when drug usage has become a part of who you are?

To begin, take a break from all influences of drugs. This means friends that indulge, music that makes you want to turn up, or situations that would encourage drug usage. This gives you a chance to clear your mind. After a week or two of clearing your mind, list all of the things that are bothering you.

What are you running from? What is disturbing you? This list is what we take to God. This list is what you pray about. Ask God to remove anyone that isn't really for you. Ask God to change and direct your path. It will be a journey but, believe me, all you have to do is take the FIRST STEP and God will do the rest. If you don't know where to begin, use these two words: BUT GOD!

Sex or No Sex: That Is the Question

It is a known fact that sex before marriage is not of God, but the temptation is REAL! When you are surrounded by friends who engage in sexual intercourse and they are telling you their stories, it is exciting. They are juicy, and you think about how that could be you! You see all the gifts she's receiving, all of the dinner dates she's going on, all the "Netflix and Chill" invites, and how she is basically "poppin".

What you don't see are the soul ties that are piling up inside of her body. You don't see all of the spiritual connections she is making once these males enter inside her HOLY TEMPLE. You don't see how they deposit parts of themselves inside of her every time she has intercourse. Every soul isn't clean! She has multiple partners so she has multiple deposits. The confusion inside of her begins to take root, because she's no longer pure.

So many people have a spiritual hold on her, that a war begins to inflict on the inside of her and she is unaware of why one minute she feels one way, and then in the next she feels another way. What she doesn't disclose is that she cries at night from feeling unwanted. She doesn't tell you that she doesn't even want to have sex, but she feels obligated like it's all she has to offer.

What she doesn't say is that she would gladly return every bag, meal, and date, for her self-respect and dignity, because now every guy she meets "expects" sex from her. What she doesn't tell you is that she pops pills, drinks lean, and smokes weed to numb the pain. She doesn't disclose that she doesn't even enjoy it anymore and barely remembers what even happens—but it's her way of remaining relevant.

Now if you knew all that would you really want to indulge? No, of course not. She's not going to tell you that, because she needs a partner in crime. What I'm not oblivious to is the fact that sex is like Pringles: "Once you pop, the fun don't stop". The question is: how many soul ties do you build up in your body before you lose yourself?

How can a man truly love you when you come with so much spiritual baggage from past sexual encounters? No matter how we, as a world, try to desensitize sexual intercourse, it is not that simple. There is no such thing as "just having sex". Physical, mental, emotional, and spiritual ties are made after intercourse happens.

This is the reason why you find yourself in situations longer than need be.

My advice would be to not have sex at all prior to marriage. Save the union for you and your husband! Is it that simple? No. If you have already started, how do you turn back? Make a decision! Decide today that you do not want to add anymore soul ties inside your body. Make a declaration that you want to begin to remove all remaining soul ties.

Ask God to guide your path. Keep yourself out of situations that will lend themselves to sexual intercourse. Be upfront with dudes when you meet them. Tell them you are not at all interested in having sex, and watch them drop like flies. Cleanse yourself spiritually. Ask God for forgiveness, and then forgive yourself! Make a list of all the sexual soul ties you've formed. Ask God to begin the journey to release you from them. Then get rid of the list. Burn it! Tear it up!

Shred it! Do whatever you feel necessary to do to let it go.

Remember that it is a journey. YOU WILL FALL, but the key to falling is NOT to stay down. Dust yourself off. Get back up and ask God to keep leading you. All you have to do is take the FIRST STEP. How do you do that? Use these two words: BUT GOD!

Coming Out the Closet

Because of the society we live in, when you see this chapter, you probably automatically begin to think of homosexuality. Well in this case, this isn't true. The closet in this chapter is just symbolism for the area in which you have spent your darkest moments. For me, I cried most of my tears in the closet. I closed the door and rocked back and forth crying.

Why, you ask? I was a lost soul and had no idea what else to do. I spent countless hours sitting in that closet crying my soul out. It was the only thing that kept me sane even though now I am knowledgeable enough to know that I was extremely depressed. For you, it may be the bed, your car, the hallway, the bathroom, or maybe even just out loud. Wherever you have been spending your darkest most depressed moments, it's time to come out.

There is nothing there but hurt, fear, depression, a lack of self-love, a loss of self-worth, and bondage. This is not what God wants or has in store for you. You have cried your last tear! There is nothing that you have done in your life that will not be forgiven by your savior. You have to accept the forgiveness. Then you have to forgive yourself.

When you are in bondage you are unaware of the damage you are causing to your spirit because the darkness has a hold of you like a frigid fall night. When you get that touch of light, it begins to illuminate throughout your soul and spark a change. You may be thinking 'how do

I get a touch of light?'. You have got to come out of the darkness!

Open that closet door and look around if need be. Make sure you are ready to make an exit. Turn around. Say farewell to the sorrow, the fear, the emotional roller coaster, the hurt, the pain, and the rejection. Make a declaration out loud say 'I'm leaving every part of this darkness where it stands'. Close the door, and step into the light. Will it all immediately end? No. I would be doing you a complete disservice to have you thinking that. What I am privileged to say is that it is the first step, and every time it begins to arise in you again, you must understand that you can no longer return to the darkness of that closet, bed, car, hallway, bathroom, or even just screaming out loud. You have already walked into the light so you have to be willing to claim your peace. You have put a spiritual lock on the place of depression so now God is your outlet.

How do you reach him when those things start to stir up again? First, don't listen to the negativity in your head! Don't allow outside forces to place negativity on you. God is a God of forgiveness and encouragement. If you get to this place all you have to do is use these two words: BUT GOD!

Alone in a crowded room

So...your mind is probably asking: "how is it possible to be alone in a crowded room?" Well, let me explain. Once that light, that we previously discussed, begins to permeate your soul, you begin a transformation. The transformation is a life-long process.

If you are a visual learner, think of the cycle of a butterfly. There are stages that the butterfly goes through before it is a graceful being soaring above, offering peace and beauty to all those in its path. That is what this process will be like, just not as quickly! Once the light begins to transform the dark, you will begin to see things differently.

The friends that you once hung out with will seem "different". It is NOT them; they are completely the same. Instead it is your mind, heart, and soul that has begun transforming. God is beginning to allow you to see the reality of situations, instead of being blinded by the darkness. The songs on the radio that you once enjoyed will begin to disrupt the very nature of who you are becoming, and you won't be able to listen to them anymore. It is no longer about the beats, you are becoming aware of the lyrical content. The things that they are saying no longer align with who you are or who you want to be.

I can remember being at this stage in my own journey of personal growth. It was so hard to let go of my "friends." I decided to go out with them to a club. When it was just us riding there, I was okay. It didn't feel as fun as it used to, but it was nice to be around some familiar faces after going through a period of being "alone". We went to a very nice club downtown. We got in for free. We didn't stand in line, and the club was in a hotel that was simply beautiful.

When we reached the rooftop where the party was located, it felt very different. It was dark, cold spirited, and only glimpses of light! EVERYONE in the club was drunk. I am very aware what happens in clubs, but this night, everyone seemed to be possessed with drunkenness. They all gyrated on each other as if they were having sex with their clothes on. Everyone seemed to be in a parallel universe as a glimpse of light would momentarily shine on the crowd. When I looked into their faces, they were totally disconnected from the world. I removed myself from the dance floor and watched everyone, and it was then that I realized that I was "alone in a crowded room".

At that moment, a girl came over and said "Hey do you wanna dance?" Just as I was about to speak, she continued with "Me and my boyfriend think you are cute and we want to take you home." I was beyond perplexed, but I was extremely delighted by the transformation that God had taken me through. I found my "friends" and told them I didn't fit into this crowd any longer. I told them to have a great night and that I would catch a cab home. They were so drunk and they agreed.

Now the issue was, I was all the way downtown in the middle of the night, and my mom's house was too far south. When I got downstairs, a cab pulled up in front of me. When I got in the cab I felt a sense of peace. The cab driver asked me where I was going and I told him. He turned around and said "I never come to this spot, and I don't normally go that far, but I will do it for you. I don't even know how I ended up here."

All I could do was praise God! I learned from that situation that, once I started feeling like I was alone in a crowded room, it was necessary for my growth to allow God to send me a new circle of friends. The period of "loneliness" that you go through during your journey is not loneliness at all! It is actually when you are in your chrysalis. God is holding you and preparing you for purpose. He is with you at all times. You just have to be in solitude so no outside forces can disrupt your preparatory stage.

If you are here or are on your way to the stage, understand that you are not alone. There is NO turning back. God has called and is preparing you for his work. It may be difficult at times, but he will send his people to comfort, console, and guide you. The first step is acknowledging and accepting that you are indeed "alone in a crowded room".

The next step is to find joy in knowing that God is preparing you for something greater. By now you should know that if the road starts getting thin and feeling rough or if you feel so alone that you cannot bear it, remember these two words: BUT GOD!

Finding the God in Me

So you've realized that you're alone in a crowded room, and God has called you to be and do greater. The first question you probably have is "now what?" That, my dear, is a very good question! Now what? You have gone through an excruciating process and parts of your chrysalis are beginning to break away. You are now awake and starting to see some of daylight. But what is next? Everyone's path is different. God is the ONLY one that has the answer to that question: "now what"?

The best advice I can give you is to find a space and time for you to be quiet. You can even transform your former place of darkness to a place of light. Quiet your spirit and ask God "now what?" God seeks to have fellowship with you. He wants to talk to you in the morning, throughout the day, and before bed. Whenever an issue arises in life, before you vent to a friend or family, vent to God! He is the only one that has the capability to offer a solution or solve the problem.

You don't have to worry about it leaving the conversation because he will never betray you. God thinks of you in the highest regards. Once you realize this, you will walk, talk, and respect yourself, as the daughter of a king that you are. If you ever need reassurance as to how important you are to God, The Bible is your road map.

The Bible clearly states: "Seek first the Kingdom of God, and all things shall be added unto you." (Matthew 6:33). What does this mean? The meaning behind this is that if you diligently look for God, everything that you are searching for, you will receive if it is in HIS WILL for your life.

How do you do that? The first step is to pray. Next, quiet yourself. Then, talk to God before anyone else, exactly how you would talk to anyone else. Ask questions. Let your requests be heard. Express your feelings and expect answers. Then encourage yourself by speaking life into every situation you enter. The power of life or death lies in your tongue. All God asks is that you commit to taking the first step. After that, he will continue his work on you. If you get lost, need help with how to pray, or what to say, where to go next, or just need guidance, you can always refer to these two words: BUT GOD!

Walking in Purpose

After you have found the God in you, the real work begins. The works that you were predestined to complete before the foundations of the Earth were laid, are now your new assignment. Don't worry—you are not too late! In all honesty, you are right on time. Your failures, triumphs, experiences, and life lessons have brought you to this place. This is the place God has made just FOR YOU! No one else can complete this part of the work, because it was tailor-made to fit only you.

You may be thinking, "what I am I supposed to be doing for your Kingdom God?" This is the most important question you may ever ask in your life. Your purpose will, not only create a plethora of wealth, it will also lead people to the Kingdom of God and his salvation! I oblige you to not take these matters into your own hands because, no matter how successful YOUR endeavors may seem, IT WILL FAIL!

It will fail because it is not what God wants for you. It will fail because it is not a part of HIS plan. It will fail because you did the leading instead of doing the following. Even if your OWN endeavors make you a substantial amount of money, you will NOT be fulfilled. Fulfillment comes solely from walking in God's purpose.

Fulfillment comes from completing God's appointed assignments. There will be various assignments along your path, and you will find no greater joy then the feeling of knowing you have done a good job! Will there be struggles? Yes. You may encounter with more obstacles then you have ever been before. Why? There are forces in the universe attempting to stop you from completing your assignment. Completion of your assignment means glory for God, and not every force in the universe is aligned with God's will. However, If God is for you then no man, woman, spirit, or demon will be able to stop you. The only thing that can hinder you, is you!

Obstacles are sent to perplex, confuse, and frustrate you. They are created to throw you off of the right path. They come to distract you from doing a mighty work, but you have to persevere. Perseverance means pushing through no matter what the circumstances in front of you may look like.

God gave me the foundation for writing this book on June 7, 2013 at 6:39 a.m. on a Friday morning before I went to work. He outlined for me 11 chapters that I was to write on in this book. As I still lay in bed, I took notes allowing God to speak to me. I started writing the book a couple of months later. I completed three chapters and I was extremely excited. I shared it with close family, a couple of friends, and then I put it on the shelf.

I would occasionally look through my journal reviewing the years' past, and I always say to myself "Man, I really need to finish that book." As the years transpired, I watched as the value of a young woman begin to deteriorate more and more. God kept quietly whispering to me "write the book." Finally, two years and six months later, I took the foundation of the book off of the shelf. I moved the book a little closer to my view, but I let it sit up for another month before I began to write again.

Finally, after speaking with a friend who was finally publishing a book she had been writing, I told her "I started writing the book again." She was elated and when I told her the title that God had given me a few days earlier, her response was "Girl, I'm going to tell you this: you betta hurry up, because that was just the topic of a book someone said they were going to write in the meeting I attended."

Although it was my friend speaking to me, it was as if God lit a fire underneath me! He told me that there is no greater time than the present. He had given me all the tools, all I had to do was commit to the work. The amazing thing about walking in your purpose, is that GOD DOES THE WORK THROUGH YOU! You are just the vessel. God gave me every sentence in every place to write in this book. All I had to do was to commit to sitting down and writing. After I committed to sitting down, and saying "okay God, I am dedicating the time to your purpose", I completed the book in a weekend! God is more than willing and ready to have you walk in your purpose effortlessly if you commit to doing the work.

The first step is to verbally make a commitment. Say "God I am ready and committed to doing your work." Next, set aside time to allow God to download into you, what he would like you to do. Then, ask God for guidance as to how you are going to accomplish this assignment. Be patient. For some, this may happen overnight. For others, it may take days, weeks, months, or even years! My advice is to NOT give up! Don't ever quit! Keep revisiting the idea until God lights a spark under you in which you can no longer ignore.

Pray this prayer:

'God you have transformed me from darkness into a beacon of light. You have allowed me to go through the necessary stages to be able to stand before you today. I trust your will and your way for my life. Not only am I ready, but I am committed to fully seeing the completion of every assignment that you have given me for this life.

I am blessed and honored to be chosen by you to help establish your Kingdom. I am fully aware that the road will be narrow and uneasy, but I am up for the challenge. God, if ever I want to turn back, please keep me focused on you. Please allow me to continuously walk in love, peace, and purpose. Let me be aware at all times that you cannot be stopped, therefore, when I am walking in my

God defined purpose, I cannot be stopped. I cannot give up! And I will not quit! You are with me and in me at all times, and when I am no longer carrying myself you have me in your arms. I declare all of this by the faith you instilled in me, in Jesus mighty name, Amen!'

If ever you get lost and cannot find your way, always remember these two words that will guide you along your journey:

www.ingramcontent.com/pod-product-compliance
Lightning Source LLC
Chambersburg PA
CBHW070551300426
44113CB00011B/1863